PIRATES WITH THE

By

Ian Gilmour

PIRATES WITH THEIR PANTS DOWN

All the characters and events in this book are fictitious, and any resemblance to actual persons living or dead is purely coincidental.

All rights reserved. No part of this publication may be reproduced, stored in a retrieval system or transmitted in any form or by any means, electronic, mechanical, photo copying, recording, or otherwise, without the prior permission of the publisher.

Copyright © Ian Gilmour 2017

PIRATES WITH THEIR PANTS DOWN
CONTENTS

Acknowledgements

Introduction

Chapter 1	Piracy and the Slave Trade
Chapter 2	The Wicked ways of Lady Sarah
Chapter 3	The Black Witch of Bodcombe
Chapter 4	The Rise and Fall of Jonny Jet
Chapter 5	Sir Ramble Bumble-Mumble

Acknowledgements

Many thanks to friends from the Mason's Arms in Odcombe and the Old Barn Club in Yeovil for their good humoured advice on the contents and characters in the story.
Kevin, Sarah, Pete and Trina

Title
PIRATES WITH THEIR PANTS DOWN
By
Ian Gilmour

PIRATES WITH THEIR PANTS DOWN

Introduction

This is the story of the life and times of a pirate family called Mumble. The Mumble family have over the years led very colourful and varied lifestyles. There have been dangerous and amusing times, but there is a dark and sinister side to the Mumble family, this will become apparent in the various chapters of the book. The story begins in the year 1710 when the infamous pirate and slave trader, Captain Kevin Grumble-Mumble, was sailing the high seas and conducting his dastardly business.

Chapter 1

Piracy and the Slave Trade

Captain Kevin Grumble-Mumble was on the poop deck of his ship, "The Scuttled Pig." The day before, the ship and crew had attacked a Spanish merchant ship carrying rum, spices and some passengers.

The Spanish crew had put up fierce resistance to the attack, and paid for this with their lives. When any ship's crew did not surrender immediately, Captain Mumble and his men ruthlessly slaughtered them without mercy. They had captured the women passengers along with the cargo the Spanish ship was carrying. Now it was time for the crew to have some fun and a tot or two of rum.

"Bring up the women," orders the captain to his first mate, Ever Ready-Neddy.

"Aye aye captain, ah wull jist go doon and get them the noo."

The captain then calls out to his crew. "We'll play the old seafaring game; Cock it or Walk it." The crew give out a great roar, "Cock it or Walk it," they shout.

On hearing this call, Tom the cabin boy shoots up the rigging like a rat up a drainpipe, not stopping until he had reached the safety of the crow's nest.

The object of this seafaring game was that a captive would have their hands tied behind their back and made to walk half way along the plank overhanging the side of the ship. The captive had a choice, after the shout of, "Cock it or Walk it," the poor unfortunate person could either, walk forward off the end of the plank into shark-infested waters and probably certain death, or walk backwards along the plank and "dock" onto an erect sailor at the ships end of the plank.

The women prisoners are now on deck; there are twelve of them in all, well-dressed and about twenty to forty years of age, with one old woman of about eighty years old.

"Ah've brought the lassies and the auld crone up for the pokin," said Ever-Ready-Neddy.

The captain addresses the women and explains the rules of the game. One of the women speaks out.

"I am a member of the German Royal Family, and you will all be hunted down like the dogs you are if any harm comes to me or any of the other women you have made prisoners."

"And who might you be?" asks the captain.

"I am the Countess Irena Arschloch, and the other women are my close family and staff."

The captain laughs aloud. "You can go first then, your Majesty, and I will be waiting for your return."

The crew roar with laughter. Ever Ready-Neddy ties her hands behind her back, the captain then prods her along with the end of his cutlass until she reaches the middle of the plank. He then shouts out. "Cock it or Walk it!" The crew repeat the shout with great gusto.

The Countess turns her head towards her friends and relatives on board the ship. "Farewell, and to hell with the pirate scum." She then continues to walk towards the end of the plank.

Ever Ready-Neddy calls out in panic. "She's goan tae walk aff the end and droon."

The captain shouts out to Ragheed the Turd from Turdistan. "Ragheed, go and bring her back aboard, she's too valuable a cargo to be eaten by the sharks." Ragheed runs along the plank and catches the countess as she is about to drop off the end. He quickly drags her back aboard ship.

The captain speaks to his crew. "There's been a change of plan; the women will be confined below decks and we'll be sure to get a huge price for such valuable stock; that is, if they are in good condition." The crew protest loudly and Ever Ready-Neddy speaks out.

"Captain Mumble sir, the men have nay had any pokin fur month's noo, wull ye no reconsider?"

The captain thinks for a minute, he does not want to have a mutiny on his hands, but he still has to maintain discipline, and command the respect of his crew. "Very well, if they must, the crew can have the old woman to poke." The old woman smiles and slips her false wooden teeth into a pocket in her clothing. She calls out. "I'm too old and frail to walk the plank; I'll just go with the poking instead." The crew all groan and give the thumbs down sign.

A crew member "Peg leg Pete," speaks out. "We don't want the old hag, we want the other women." The captain is now getting a bit worried and speaks to the crew. "We will arrive at Bunga Island tomorrow, where there are plenty of young women.

You can poke away all week if you wish. This seems to calm the crew down; except for Peg leg Pete, who still complains.

"We've waited long enough, we want the women now!" Captain Kevin Grumble-Mumble moves like lightning, and with one swift slash of his cutlass, he cuts off Peg leg Pete's good leg. Blood spurts from the stump of the screaming sailor as his lifeblood drains away and he dies in agony. The captain throws the lifeless body and severed leg over the side of the ship. As soon as they hit the water, sharks voraciously feed on the remains.

"Now, has anyone else got any complaints?" The crew all remain silent. The captain gives an order. "Neddy, take the women below." There was no reply from, or any sight of Ever Ready-Neddy. Earlier his "shifty darting eyes," had spotted the old woman smile and put her false wooden teeth into her pocket. During the ensuing melee, he had taken her below deck. Tom the cabin boy shouts out from the crow's nest. "Land Ahoy!"

Captain Mumble looks through his telescope. He sees the shoreline of Bunga Island. "Look lively me hearties, and hoist the mainsail, Bunga Island is now in sight. "Ragheed, take the women below deck and let's make haste." Ragheed the Turd tells the women to follow him down to the brig. He looks through the iron bars and sees Ever Ready-Neddy and the old woman indulging in behaviour of the grossest kind.

"You dirty little heathen," shouts Ragheed to Ever Ready-Neddy. "The captain is looking for you; you had better get back up on deck." The old woman puts her false wooden teeth back into her mouth. Neddy reports to the captain. The old woman follows behind him.

"Where have you been? I needed you here earlier."

"Sorry captain sur, the auld crone was feelin a wee bit faint, so I took her below decks so she could lay doon fur a bit. Then ah slipped and knocked ma heed against a beam and became unconscious."

"Is there no end to your bullshit, Neddy? Help the crew get this ship moving at full speed. A warning is heard from the crow's nest. "Ship approaching from the south west" shouts out Tom. A whistling noise, followed by the sound of splitting wood follows, as a cannonball smashes into the upper deck of the ship.

"Man the guns, we are under attack," shouts the captain. He looks through his spyglass and sees it is a Spanish warship approaching fast. "Bollocks" curses the captain and orders his men to return fire. The captain feels a searing pain in his left arm. He looks down and sees a set of false wooden teeth embedded deeply with blood pouring from the wound.

He screams out and sees the headless body of the old woman lying on the deck beside him. A cannonball had taken her head off and her false teeth had shot out and ended up in the captain's arm.

Before the crew have time to open fire on the Spanish ship, it suddenly explodes and a massive fireball fills the horizon. When the smoke clears there is no sign of the Spanish ship, it was gone. The crew give out a massive cheer. The ship that had sunk the Spanish vessel is now approaching. It has the pirate skull and crossbones flag flying aloft.

Captain Mumble raises his spyglass and sees the familiar sight of his friend and fellow pirate, Captain Davy One Ball-Crump on the deck of his ship, The Bone Scutter.

The Bone Scutter is now alongside the Scuttled Pig, but there is a strange silence from the new arrival. Captain Mumble fears the worse but it is too late, he sees the lifeless body of Captain Crump tied to the mast pole. British marines appear on the deck and open fire with their rifles mowing down the crew of the Scuttled Pig, who were standing on the deck overlooking the arriving ship. A boarding party of British sailors attack the ship. Deadly hand to hand combat ensues. Captain Kevin Grumble-Mumble is fighting fiercely with his cutlass and knife.

The attacking force greatly outnumbers the crew that are left after the initial onslaught by the marines. Soon the fight is over and only ten men remain alive from a crew of one hundred and twenty of the Scuttled Pig.

This had been an elaborate trap by the British Navy who had earlier captured the Bone Scutter and destroyed her crew.

Captain Mumble, Ragheed the Turd and Ever Ready-Neddy along with Tom the cabin boy and six of the deck hands are the only crew members to survive. Ever Ready-Neddy had been found down in the Brig hiding along with the previously captured women. Standing on the deck of the Scuttled Pig looking down on the remaining captured crew… who were now tied up and in chains, was the infamous British captain John Dread.

"At last I have captured the scourge of the open seas," roars Captain Dread. "You and your remaining crew will be taken back to Great Britain and hanged, drawn and quartered, and I will take the greatest of pleasures in watching the event. The cabin boy will be spared.

Captain Mumble spits in the direction of Captain Dread. A rotting mixture of blood and saliva hits him and runs down his face.

Captain Dread curses, "You filthy pirate bastard." He moves toward Captain Mumble and kicks him in the face. He is now mad with rage. "I've changed my mind, hang them now," orders Captain Dread. Ever Ready Neddy screams out in fear. "Ah don't want tay be hanged, ah did nay dae any of the fighting, ah wis doon in the Brig."

"Take the women below, they won't want to watch this," orders Captain Dread. "Yes, we do want to watch," shouts out the smiling Countess Irena Arschloch. "Very well, hang the Scotsman first" orders the captain. The crew members drag the now screaming Ever Ready-Neddy over to the yard arm where a rope with the hangman's noose on the end is waiting.

One by one the remaining crew of the Scuttled Pig are hanged, Captain Kevin Grumble Mumble being the last one to see the end of the rope.

The years pass and the surviving members of the Mumble family prosper and now live a life of high living with not a small amount of scandal ensuing. The story continues with more interesting Mumbles exploits.

Chapter 2

The Wicked ways of Lady Sarah

Lady Sarah Tumble-Mumble is in the hayloft above the stables cavorting with her Uncle Ivan Fumble-Mumble.

"Faster Uncle Ivan, faster," shouts Sarah to her humping uncle. Sarah tightens and twists the grip on her knickers that are around Ivan's neck. Sweat is pouring from his brow and he is in danger of passing out. He has got to get Lady Sarah to release her strangling grip of the knickers. He delivers a hard slap to the side of her face, which causes Sarah to squeal out, release her hold on the knickers. He then quickly finishes the poking.

"You are a 'wicked' girl to take advantage of your old uncle like that. I've a mind to tell your husband about your tricks."

"Tell him if you like, you old twat! You're not my real uncle anyway."

Ivan is getting himself dressed and picks up Sarah's knickers. He then uses them to wipe the sweat from his brow and to clean off the end of his gun.

"You dirty bastard," screams Lady Sarah and kicks out with both feet knocking Uncle Ivan out of the hayloft, where he lands on a steaming pile of horseshit and straw. Lady Sarah makes her way back to the manor house and goes in through the tradesman's entrance. She enters the kitchen where she sees Bill the butcher standing with his apron lifted.

On her knees, with her head under the apron is Lisa the pantry maid, indulging in, some kind of sausage tasting, well that was the reply from the butcher when Lady Sarah asked him what was going on.

The pantry maid scuttles out of the kitchen and Bill the butcher lowers his apron. He then asks Lady Sarah if she requires any extra meat for next week's dinner party.

"Yes, thank you Bill, double the order, and four more chickens please." Bill writes down the extra order and asks. "Stuffing mi Lady?"

"Yes, Bill and 'right away' if you please." The butcher looks up from his notebook and is startled at the sight in front of him. Lying on the kitchen table is Lady Sarah with her skirt hoisted up around her waist. Bill is delighted and lifts his apron for the second time that day.

Uncle Ivan Fumble-Mumble arrives back at the manor house and staggers in through the front door. He hears voices coming from the games room and looks in through the partially open door. He sees Lord Rodger Fiddler-Mumble with his plus fours around his ankles and his shirtfront lifted. In front of him with his shirttail lifted and bent over the snooker table, is Harold the footman.

Uncle Ivan calls out. "Potting the brown again Rodger?" Lord Rodger is startled and jumps back in fright. "Can't you knock, you silly old twat, and what the hell happened to you? You look like you've been knocked down by a horse and dung cart." Lord Rodger lowers the footman's shirttail and sends him out of the room.

"I was looking at the horses in the stables, when I slipped and fell into a pile of horseshit and straw," replies Ivan.

"Are you sure you've not been shagging my wife?"

"What the hell makes you think that?" Asks Ivan

"Well for starters, that looks like a pair of her silk knickers hanging out of your pocket, and for seconds, you have knicker elastic burns around your neck, no doubt caused by a dangerous practice favoured by Lady Sarah. Go and get yourself cleaned up, we'll discuss this later."

Lord Rodger makes his way to the kitchen. He wants to check if the cook has returned from her visit to a relative. He enters the kitchen and sees Lady Sarah and Bill the butcher on the kitchen table. He calls out. "Have you no damned shame or decency woman? Food has to be prepared on that table." Bill the butcher lowers his apron and beats a hasty retreat out of the manor house.

"Where is the cook?"

"She hasn't returned from her visit yet, replies Sarah. She is getting down from the table when Lord Rodger smiles wryly and speaks out. "Stay where you are my dear." He then raises his shirtfront and continues where the butcher had left off.

Rachel the cook returns and cries out at the humping couple. "Begging your pardon, but food has to be prepared on that table, and it's only three hours until dinner is served." Lord Rodger laughs and lowers his shirtfront. Lady Sarah also laughs hysterically as she gets down from the table.

"I'll just go upstairs and get changed for dinner," says Sarah. She then departs from the kitchen.

Rodger says to the cook. "Can you set another place for dinner Rachel? My cousin, 'Captain James Cockhandy' may arrive either later today or tomorrow morning, better to be prepared."

"Right you are mi Lord; how long is the captain staying for?"

"He has a week's leave from his Regiment, but after Lady Sarah gets her hands on him, I'll be surprised if he's here for more than two days." Both the cook and Lord Rodger laugh out loudly.

"What regiment does the captain serve in, mi Lord?"

"He serves in the famous Royal Foreskin Fusiliers, whose motto is, *Who Pulls Back Wins*." Lord Rodger looks at the cook and smiles. "You're looking very sexy today Rachel, and that's a nice short tweed skirt you're wearing." The cook knows what's on his mind, and raises her skirt. Roger smiles again and lifts his shirtfront for the third time that day.

Lady Sarah is in her room getting dressed for dinner. She hears noises outside in the courtyard. She looks out of the window and sees three riders dressed in military uniforms. Lady Sarah has never met Captain James before, as he had been overseas with the army when she married Lord Rodger. The soldiers dismount and she sees Lord Rodger shake hands with one of the men. Lady Sarah opens the window to hear their conversation.

"Welcome James, and who are the two fellows with you? I thought you would be on your own."

"Sorry Rodger, but my leave has been cancelled, we are here on official business. You will have to come back to Parliament tomorrow, my men and I will escort you. There are important matters to be resolved. These are dangerous times and the King requires your presence.

"Very well, we will have dinner tonight and set off in the morning." Rodger summons his butler. "Bumstead, take the captain and his men up to the guest rooms. Gentlemen, dinner will be at eight sharp, the dinner gong will sound five minutes before."

Bumstead the butler shows the captain and his men up to the guest rooms. Lady Sarah hurries out to the hallway and discreetly watches which rooms Captain James and his men go into. Sarah waits until all is clear and knocks on the captain's door. The door opens, Lady Sarah smiles and coyly introduces herself. "Hello, I am Sarah, Lord Rodgers wife, and you must be the famous Captain James Cockhandy."

"I am indeed, and may I say that it is a pleasure to meet such a beautiful and refined young lady."

"It will be shortly," says Lady Sarah as she enters the room and locks the door behind her.

The dinner gong sounds. The guests and family members soon arrive to take their places at the dinner table. Seated at the top of the table is Lord Rodger. Opposite him is Lady Sarah, grinning like a Cheshire cat. Captain James takes his seat next to Rodger. Also at the table are the captain's men and Uncle Ivan Fumble-Mumble. Rodger speaks to the captain.

"Captain James, I can see by the red knicker elastic burns around your neck that you are already acquainted with my wife." The captain is speechless and looks knackered. His eyes are sticking out of his head like dog's bollocks and his face is pale and drawn. He tries to speak, but no sound comes from his mouth. Lady Sarah had sorted him out good and proper and nearly killed him by the look of things.

Lady Sarah laughs and throws a roast potato, which bounces off the head of Captain James. "Cat got your tongue James?" asks Sarah.

Uncle Ivan is rubbing at his own neck, which still bears the red burn marks inflicted by Lady Sarah earlier. He starts to speak. "Nice weather we're having today."

"Shut up you silly old twat," says Sarah. She throws another potato, which bounces off the head of Uncle Ivan. He stands up and protests loudly.

"I've had enough of your hospitality Rodger, and that wife of yours should be horsewhipped. She is a danger to man and beast. Look at the mess she's made of the captain, and I don't feel too clever myself.

"Don't take things so seriously Uncle Ivan, you've had your leg over a beautiful woman, and at your age, you should be grateful," answers Lord Rodger. Another potato bounces off the side of Ivan's head. Lady Sarah laughs out again.

"That's it! I'm leaving this house and never coming back." With that, Uncle Ivan Fumble-Mumble storms off to pack his bags. This would be the last time any of them would see Ivan alive except for one person.

Later that night while he is making his way home on horseback, he sees another mounted figure stopped on the track ahead. He reins back his horse and sees the masked face of the person in front of him.

"Stand and deliver" comes the call from the ambusher pointing a pistol directly at him. He has fallen victim to a highway robber.

"What do you want?" asks Ivan.

"Your money and your life," replies the robber.

"I recognise that voice, it is you Lady Sarah!" The robber removes the mask to reveal the smiling face of Lady Sarah. She laughs aloud and Ivan reaches for his pistol. A shot is fired and a piercing scream fills the dark night. Lady Sarah is laughing aloud as she looks at the fallen figure of Uncle Ivan Fumble-Mumble. She had fired the fatal shot that hit poor Ivan between the eyes, killing him instantly. Sarah quickly removes any money Uncle Ivan had been carrying, and heads back to the Manor. She quietly puts her horse back in the stables and creeps back into the manor house. Unseen, the ever watchful Bumstead the butler has secretly observed her return, and that may be her undoing, or maybe not! The next day, Lord Rodger along with the captain and his men leave the house to meet with the king at parliament. After they had gone, Bumstead the butler approaches Lady Sarah.

"I noticed you returned home quite late last night my Lady, and I also saw the strange clothing you were wearing. However, I am sure we can arrange a special meeting for a bit of fun and games. Your secret will be safe with me. No one else needs to find out."

Sarah smiles wryly. "Very well, meet me in the stable loft in ten minutes and we will have a lovely close encounter. Bumstead smiles and scratches his parts.

Lady Sarah is waiting in the loft when the butler enters the stable. "Up here," shouts out Lady Sarah. Bumstead climbs up the ladder and smiles when he sees the naked form of Sarah smiling and kneeling in front of him. His smile turns to a look of fear as he sees the pitchfork she is holding. Sarah drives the pitchfork into the butler's neck killing him instantly. He drops to the ground where Lady Sarah drags his lifeless body over to the pig pit. The pigs make short work of devouring Bumstead, nothing is left.

Time goes by and Lady Sarah has now had a daughter who is named Triana Grumpy-Mumble. The child grows up quickly and it is soon apparent that she is possessed by evil. The final straw comes after she strangles her grandmother for calling her a witch. She is sent to live with an aunt in the village of Bodcombe.

Chapter 3

The Black Witch of Bodcombe

Josiah Jenson the "Vicar of Bodcombe" is in the village church conducting the Sunday service. He speaks with a raised voice as he addresses the congregation.

"There are 'dark and evil deeds' being performed in this village that will have to end. Witchcraft, sorcery, and other abominations are taking place. Anyone found to be taking part, or associating in any way with these practices will face severe punishment."

"Bollocks," shouts the vicar as he wipes the bird droppings from his head. Directly above him, perched on the rafters is a raven. The door of the church flies open. Standing in the doorway dressed in a black cape with her face hidden by a veil, is Triana Grumpy- Mumble, the "Black Witch of Bodcombe." She is holding a rope with a hangman's noose on the end. The congregation cower in fear at the caped figure.

The vicar calls out. "Be gone from this sacred place you, old witch." A cackling laugh comes from Triana as she points her finger at the vicar.

Suddenly the vicar appears to be paralysed and in a trance, as does the entire congregation. The vicar cannot move or speak as the black witch approaches him. She places the noose over his head and secures it around his neck. The vicar appears to float behind her as she leads him up to the top of the tower. The black witch secures the other end of the rope around one section of the turret facing the churchyard. She then mumbles and chants some magical words.

The spell is lifted and the congregation are now able to move and speak again. They are all in shock and scared out of their minds. "Let's get out of here," shouts one of them. They all make their way out of the church and see a dark shadow in front of them. As they look up above the shadow, they see the vicar standing motionless on the turret at the top of the tower. Standing behind him is the Black Witch.

"I return your vicar to you; catch." Then she pushes him off the end of the turret. The vicar drops about ten feet before stopping with a jolt as the noose tightens. The congregation scream as they see the hanged body swaying in the wind. Panic ensues as they scatter and run to their homes. The villagers lock and bar all their doors and windows. Dark times lie ahead in this cursed place.

It is midnight and standing in the middle of the street is the Black Witch surrounded by her followers. She and all the others in the circle are naked. Triana Grumpy-Mumble points to the sky, she chants some words of evil. This is black magic and sorcery in action. The clouds part and a red mist falls on the village. The wind increases as the mist rushes and forces its way into the houses. Through the cracks in doors and windows, the mist invades. Screaming and crying continue as the villagers try in vain to avoid the choking gas. They try blocking up any spaces under the doors, floors and windows, but their efforts are to no avail.

Soon all is quiet in the village, the villagers appear to be asleep or dead, except for the Black Witch and her coven. A village elder, "Jack Daw," is on his knees in the centre of the circle. Triana slits his throat in ritual sacrifice. What follows is an orgy of sex and depravity. The male members are all taking it in turns to have sex with the black witch. This continues throughout the night until daybreak.

The red mist is gone, but something strange had occurred. The Bodcombe villagers have awoken from a deep sleep, but none of them can remember anything about the previous day. John the woodchopper speaks to his wife. "Jane, did we go to the church service yesterday? I can't remember a thing about Sunday."

"It's funny you should say that, for I can't remember anything either."

"That's very strange Jane, were we drinking that scrumpy cider again?"

"I don't know wooden-top, I told you I can't remember anything at all about yesterday." The same thing was happening throughout the village, no one could remember a thing about the previous day. Egor the gardener is cutting the grass in the church graveyard when he sees Pete the blacksmith coming up the path.

"How be doing Pete?"

"Not bad Egor, what's the latest news then?"

Egor scratches his head in thought. "Well now, it seems the vicar has disappeared, he's been missing for the last three days, he's not at home, neither has he left a message with anyone. Even his wife doesn't know where he is. He seems to have vanished into thin air." Pete voiced an opinion. "He's probably run off with some old slapper." Both men roar with laughter. Another person approaches along the path. It is old "Davy Doom," a local rambler and bird watcher. He starts talking to the other two men when the piecing sound of a raven is heard coming from the church tower.

Davy raises his binoculars. Below the raven, he notices a new gargoyle beside the others that had been up there for many years. He gasps for breath.

"What's up?" asks Egor.

"Look for yourself," replies Davy Doom. Egor looks through the binoculars and cries out. "Bloody Hell! It looks like the stone head of the vicar, with a look of fear and terror on his face. I think something evil has happened here." The three men decide to go down to the village pub to discuss the matter further. As they enter the Masonic Arms pub, Tim the friendly landlord greets them.

"How be hanging?" asks Tim. "Fair to middlin," answers Egor. But strange things have been happening in the village, the vicar has disappeared and there's another gargoyle that looks like him on the church wall." The others shake their heads.

"Bloody witchcraft and black magic if you ask me," says Pete. Davy Doom and Egor agree.

"Anyway, three pints of rough cider please landlord," orders Pete the blacksmith. He is paying for the drinks when the door flies open and a well-known lady of the night, Betty Swallocks enters the pub.

"Out," shouts Tim to Betty. "You're not coming in here hawking your mutton, go on, be off with you."
Pete intervenes. "Come on now Tim, its Christmas time and I'm sure Betty will behave herself today." The others also plead Betty's case. Betty also says that she has only come in for a quiet drink and will not be hawking today. "Very well, says Tim, but the first sign of any nonsense, then out you go."

A loud crashing noise is heard coming from the far end of the bar. They all look up to see Mary Hinge the chambermaid lying on the floor. She had been taking a full chamber pot out for emptying, when she tripped and the pot shattered covering her with the contents. Poor Mary let out a blood-curdling scream and ran off in the direction of the garden. Dandy Dave the cellar man has come in to see what had happened. "What's going on dahlings?" asks Dave.

Tim the friendly landlord explains what had occurred. Dandy Dave is standing there listening with one hand on hip and the other limp wristed hand holding a white handkerchief." Dandy Dave giggles and waves his white handkerchief as he tiptoes back to the cellar. Egor is secretly checking his money to see if he can afford a round of drinks and a meeting with Betty Swallocks later.

Pete the blacksmith speaks out. "I believe that the witch Triana is behind this entire vicar disappearing thing, with her secret meetings and black magic goings on. I am telling you we will have to do something about her or we will all be doomed.

"Burn her out, I say," shouts Egor. They all discuss the matter further, getting more and more pissed up on the cider. A loud cracking noise is heard followed by a thud as Davy Doom is knocked off his stool by a blow from Tim's baton. Tim had spotted him pressing a shiny shilling into the hand of prostitute Betty Swallocks.

"I told you, no mutton hawking in here!" shouts Tim. While all the commotion is taking place in the pub, the black witch is heating up a metal poker until it is white hot. In a cage in the middle of her barn is the terrified vicar of Bodcombe. He had not been killed, but had been kept alive and secretly taken to Triana's lair. In a circle around the cage are the evil followers of the black witch.
Triana screams with laughter as she presses the 'glowing white' hot poker against the ear of the vicar. He screams out in agony as the others laugh and chant their evil words.

Meanwhile back in the Masonic Arms, Davy Doom is back on his stool, rubbing the lump on his head and bleating that he had only given Betty the money to buy a drink. "Shut up," says Egor, as he knocks him off his stool again with a good aimed punch. Tim then suggests a way to get rid of the Black Witch.

"The only way to get rid of her is by fire, but first we will have to stop her using magic powers against us. I have brought this large magical rivet back from the deepest African jungle. It is made of gold and was used by the Umbollock tribe to kill witches and the like. The rivet is thrown against the witch where it attaches itself to the body paralysing the person immediately and rendering any witches powers useless. The witch is then burned and consumed in the flames.

Egor speaks out. "Right! are we all agreed, we will give Triana Grumpy-Mumble the golden rivet, burn her to ashes and get rid of her evil from our village. We will also have to get rid of her followers."

Tim speaks again. "I will give the black witch the golden rivet while the rest of you shoot her followers, and then we will burn the lot of them. Now this is the plan!

The black witch sees the flames from the burning cross, she screams aloud and orders her coven to follow her towards the burning cross. The black witch points at the men carrying the cross and chants her evil words of sorcery. The fiery cross flies up into the air. At the same time Tim releases the golden rivet which attaches itself to Triana Grumpy-Mumble.

She lets out a blood curdling scream as her powers are no more and she becomes motionless and frozen like a statue. The cross bearer and his men then shoot the rest of the witch's followers. The black witch and her entire coven are then set alight and consumed by the flames.

The vicar is released, the village is rid of the evil brought by the black witch, peace and tranquillity are restored to the village of Bodcombe.

Chapter 4

The Rise and Fall of Jonny Jet

Jonny Jet Mumble was furious when he read the note and discovered that two of his most trusted associates had betrayed him and had disappeared along with ten million pounds worth of his diamonds and other precious gems. "Death to the thieving bastards when I get a hold of them," roared Jonny in a rage. He grabbed hold of the messenger who had delivered the bad news and threw him out of a window.

As the unfortunate fellow dropped from the twenty fourth floor to the ground below, there wasn't much hope. Jonny was not over fond of anyone who brought him bad news. The authorities were also getting a bit concerned, as this would bring the total to three messengers in a week found splattered on the concrete ground at the same location.

Jonny Jet was deciding on his next course of action when there was a loud knocking followed by the shout, "Police, open the door." Jonny opened the door and the officers rushed into the room.

"What the hell is going on?" asked Jonny. "A messenger has been found dead at the foot of the building," replied one of the officers. The other policeman was looking out of the window at the street below when he summoned his fellow officer over to the window.

Jonny saw the two men whispering to each other and he also noticed a letter sticking out of the corner of the window frame. The policemen had also spotted the letter and were slowly reaching for their guns.

  Jonny knew the game was up and like a flash of lightening he rushed at the officers with a broom and fired them out of the window to their demise.
A woman in the room below had been looking out of her window and saw the screaming uniformed men fall to their doom. "What the hell was that?" asked her partner. "It must be the Flying Squad," replies the woman.

  Jonny hears a noise from behind, he turns around and sees one of the cleaners standing in the corridor looking through the open doorway She had witnessed the killing of the police officers. She pleads with Jonny. "I won't say anything to anyone, please let me go on my way."

  "Don't worry about it," says Jonny as he puts a re-assuring hand around the back of her neck. He looks around the corridor and sees that there is nobody else in sight. With a tightening of his grip and the heel of his other hand under the woman's chin, Jonny forces her head up with a slight twisting motion, breaking her neck and killing her instantly. Jonny has to act fast to get out of this mess. He drags the unfortunate woman into his room and closes the door. He makes a telephone call to an associate, Bronco the hit man, for help. "Bronco, I need some urgent assistance to get out of this hotel, the police have the place surrounded and are checking all the rooms." He explains what has occurred.

  Bronco replies. "No worries, I will be there shortly with Tomahawk Tom and Mad Mary from Macedonia. Can you make it to the basement car park?"

"Yes, I have an idea, meet me at the service lift in the car park."

Jonny decides to disguise himself as the cleaner to make his escape. He is no stranger to women's clothing and quickly strips the cleaner and dresses in her clothes.

He then drags her lifeless body over to the window. With one hand around her neck and the other at the crotch, with grip and action like a ten-pin bowler, he launches her out of the open window.

Tomahawk Tom is lying back handcuffed to the four-poster bed and smiling. Bouncing astride him is Juicy Juliana. The door flies open and Bronco rushes in. "There's no time for that now, we have an urgent mission to rescue Jonny Jet." The bonking duo appear to be oblivious of Bronco's presence. He takes off his belt, the thick leather bites into the flesh of Juicy Juliana. She lets out a squeal, more in pleasure than in pain and carries on humping with greater gusto.

Tomahawk Tom shouts out. "Hit me with the belt as well."

"Bollocks to this," shouts Bronco, drawing and aiming his gun. He issues an order. "Stop now, one, two." Juliana screams and jumps off Tomahawk Tom, frantically trying to undo the hand cuffs. She knows only too well that Bronco does not bluff and always kills after the count of three if he does not get his way.

They are soon on their way to rescue Jonny Jet, but first they have to pick up Mad Mary. They stop at the arranged place. Bronco sees Mary beside the lifeless body of a traffic warden pinned by a bolt through his neck to a telegraph pole. "What the hell happened here," asks Bronco.

"The warden said I was parked in a restricted area, so I thought I would try out my new exploding bolt gun on him to restrict his tongue wagging."

Mad Mary then shrieked with laughter. "I punched his ticket for sure." Again, wild laughter is heard from the mad one.

"Get in the van, quickly," shouts Bronco. Mad Mary turns and fires an exploding bolt into her stolen parked car which is immediately engulfed in flames.

Meanwhile back at the hotel Jonny Jet has managed to get down to the basement via the service lift. He looks out and sees that the basement area has police swarming all over the place. He closes the service lift door and quickly tapes the controls to stop the lift from operating and the door opening. The armed police guards at the entrance to the basement car park see the approaching laundry van and one guard raises his hand to stop the vehicle.

As the van stops, Mad Mary fires a bolt from her new toy into the neck of one guard killing him instantly, at the same time Tomawk Tom strikes with deadly result. His tomahawk is buried deep into the neck of the other guard. They hide the bodies out of site. They then drive down to the service lift.

There are many armed police moving around, some are going up the stairway and others using the public lift. There is also one trying to get the service lift to work. The van doors open. Mad Mary and Juliana jump out and spray the area with their machine guns mowing down all in sight. Tomahawk Tom has thrown a grenade into the stairway and throws in a smoke bomb to follow. Bronco has slit the throat of the policeman trying to get into the service lift. He jams the public lift. Jonny Jet opens the service lift door and is quickly into the van.

The others also get into the van after decimating the area. The van races out of the car park and onto the open highway. Bronco shouts out, laughing at the same time. "The plan worked a treat, well done everybody." "Yes, thanks everyone, well done indeed," says Jonny Jet. Jonny Jet lives to fight another day. He continues with his mission to find the men who stole his diamonds. The years pass and Jonny leaves a trail of destruction with many dead during his quest to track down the thieves.

    Jonny's private jet is flying past a hovering helicopter over open water when heat guided missiles are fired from the helicopter. The missiles hit their target and the jet explodes in a ball of fire. The circling helicopter pilot watches as the remains of the jet fall into the shark infested waters below. The pilot who had shot down Jonny Jet Mumbles aeroplane was none other than his friend Bronco the hit man. He had found the men who stole Jonny's diamonds and had done a deal with them for four million pounds to hit Jonny Jet. It looks like another Mumble has bit the dust. Honour among thieves, I think not!

    The side door of the helicopter is slid open and two bodies with bolts through their necks fall to the sea below. They were the two associates who had stolen Jonny Jet's diamonds. "Fair's fair," said Mad Mary as she closed the door of the helicopter. She looks at the open suitcase containing Jonny Jets stolen diamonds and laughs aloud as does Juicy Juliana, Tomahawk Tom and Bronco the hit man. Laughing loudest of all was Bronco's co-pilot in the helicopter who had fired the missiles that downed the jet. "The plan worked a treat," said Jonny Jet.

Chapter 5

Sir Ramble Bumble-Mumble

The great explorer Ramble Bumble-Mumble was tracking through the jungle in search of a lost aircraft that had disappeared some years ago. The plane was believed to have crashed into the jungle with the loss of the crew and a cargo of cash and gold. Despite numerous searches nothing was ever found.

This is a place of great danger where no other explorers venturing into the jungle have ever returned from. Ramble hears a noise and dives to the ground as an arrow flies overhead. More arrow fly past in his vicinity as he circles in the direction of where the arrows were coming from.

He hears voices up ahead and approaches with caution. In sight are now three near naked painted warriors of a fearsome tribe who inhabit the lands around this area. He knows they kill, indulge in torture and eat their victims. His trusty jungle knife slashes open the throat of the first tribesman and his silencer pistol takes out the other two with a shot each to the head. He continues onwards with his perilous journey.

Ramble is now going through a valley with steep sides. He is low on water and needs to find some soon. Up ahead he sees a trickle of water dropping off the side of the valley wall. He sticks his head under the water and takes in a mouthful. He spits out the putrid liquid. "Bollocks" he curses under his breath as he looks up and sees a painted warrior pissing over the ridge. This is where the water was coming from. Ramble backtracks a bit and climbs up to the top of the ridge, He creeps up on the pissing tribesman and clubs him unconscious. After he has tied the warrior up he waits till the man awakens.

"How many of your tribe are in this area," Ramble asks the warrior in his own language. He had learned this gibberish over the many years travel through the jungle.

"Go take a hike" replies the tribesman. Ramble Bumble-Mumble is taken aback by the poshness of the heathen and gives him a slap. I won't ask again and if you don't answer you will die." The warrior spat in the direction of Ramble, who responded by driving his trusty knife through the cheeky fellow's tongue and out of the back of his neck. Sir Ramble shoved the lifeless body over the ridge and continued with his journey taking the warriors supply of water with him.

Many weeks have passed and it was just by chance that Ramble saw the glint of light coming from a dense part of the jungle. He hacked his way through with his trusty machete and after many hours reached the source of the light. In front of him completely covered in dense foliage was the missing aircraft he was seeking. The glint of light had come from a small uncovered part of a window the sun had cast a reflection off. Sir Ramble had been at the right place at the right time.

Sir Ramble returned to Britain a very wealthy man. When he was asked if he had discovered the aircraft with the gold and cash, he always answered, "no."

To
Ian
from

Ian ~~Hilson~~

Happy
Birthday

Printed in Great Britain
by Amazon